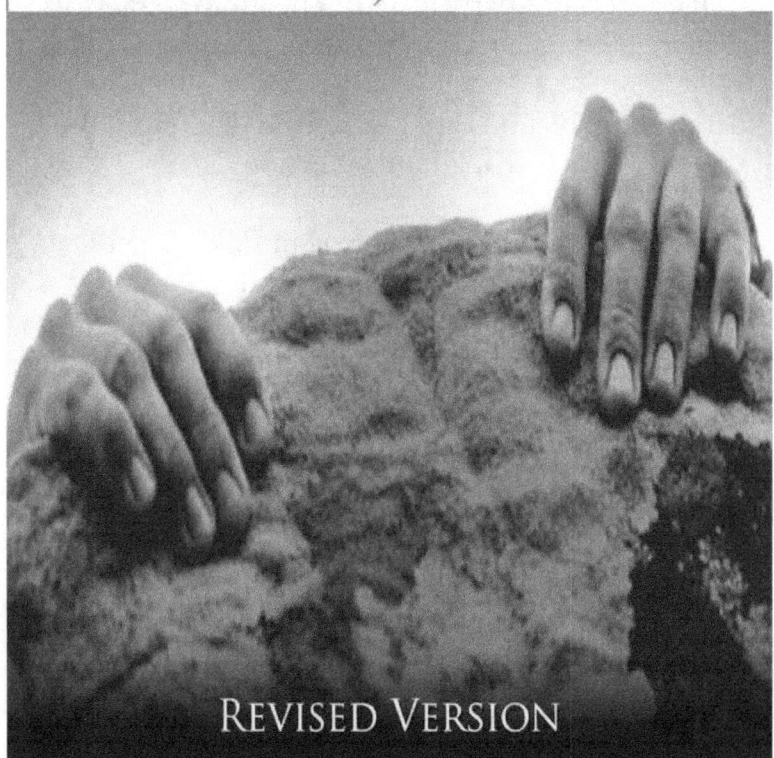

©2019 by Tammie J. Traylor

All rights reserved, including the right to reproduce this book or portions thereof in any form whatsoever by author. No part of this book may be reproduced, scanned, or distributed in any print or electronic form without permission.
Please do not participate or encourage piracy of copyrighted materials in violation of author's rights.

Scripture quotations are taken from The Holy Bible, King James Version

Library of Congress Cataloging-in Publication Data
ISBN-978-0-9974047-1-5

Tammie J. Traylor (text)
Beyond the Stone

Published by Writing in Faith LLC
Baton Rouge

<u>IAmWritinginfaith.com</u>

Beyond the Stone

Can You Believe Again?

By

Tammie J. Traylor

TABLE OF CONTENTS

DEDICATION.. vii

FROM THE AUTHOR.. xiii

FOREWARD... xvii

PREFACE.. xxi

1. CHAPTER ONE
   Tragedy at Bethany... 27

2. CHAPTER TWO
   Through Martha's Eyes.. 41

3. CHAPTER THREE
   Lazarus is Dead.. 59

4. CHAPTER FOUR
   Stones... 75

5. CHAPTER FIVE
   Where is Jesus?... 99

6. CHAPTER SIX
   What is Really Going On?.. 119

7. CHAPTER SEVEN
   The Shattered Heart of a Worshipper............ 129

8. CHAPTER EIGHT
   Beyond the Stone.. 139

9. CHAPTER NINE
   Come Forth!... 151

10. CHAPTER TEN
    He That Was Dead Now Lives!............................ 161

11. CHAPTER ELEVEN
    Conclusion... 171

DEDICATION

This book is dedicated to my mother, Phyllis Jackson and my father. Also, I would like to honor the memories of my two beautiful children, Carrington and Houston, who have gone to be with the Lord......

I love you!

This book tells the timeless story of Mary, Martha and Lazarus that has been read, told and interpreted many times. Yet, it has never been told quite like this. We all have issues, dreams and goals that have been in our tombs of disappointment. Out of normalcy, we have carted our jewels of destiny to the gravesite, after having watched these precious gems die in our arms, right before our very eyes. Yes, they are dead... but do they have to remain that way? How is it that something DEAD can live again? How do you restart the very heart of your destiny? There is hope! Things are not as they seem. Faith does not deny facts. However, it does bear witness with the TRUTH.

The time has finally come to revive that which you thought was lost. Now, go to that place where you laid the dead thing to rest. Remove the flowers, the pretty things that camouflage the stench of dead things and go beyond the stone.

Once the stone is removed, you won't be afraid to call forth that which was once dead to its intended state of vitality. The truth hurts, but the jolt of reality is necessary to awaken an otherwise DEAD situation.

It's amazing what you can see in the light compared to what you thought you could see in the dark! Dare to believe that it's not over until God says it's over!

FROM THE AUTHOR

It is not by coincidence that you have picked up this book. It is by divine appointment. Whether you admit it or not, you are looking for a change. You may ask, how do you know this? Well, my friend God told me so through his Word (Romans 8:19) that all of creation is waiting on a change. The birds, trees, the atmosphere, men, women, and children are all waiting for something to change. As a natural reaction, when we need something, we begin to seek out different options until we find contentment. You never start to look for something until it is time for it to manifest. It is time for change to manifest in your life. You picked up this book, expecting. You won't be disappointed.

Today is the first day of a whole new world just for you. God loved you enough to allow you to walk through the store and draw you to your deliverance, your healing, or maybe even your spiritual awakening. Your life will never be the same.

I hope you're ready. We will journey to that forgotten, hollow ground where you buried things that you dare not mention or recollect in the light. God wants to remove all of those things that have infected you and hindered you from reaching your life's potential. If you are brave enough to surrender to the hand of the Lord and hear what the Spirit has to say to you, I promise that you won't even remember the hurt when he gets through with you. All you will remember is the change.

FOREWORD

Freedom has arrived on the scene today. There are so many people today who live behind big, elaborate facades. They look so wonderful on the outside, all dressed up and squeaky clean. But, on the inside, they stink from the stench of rotten flesh. They have been hurt. So, for many years they have locked away the pain.

It's ironic that so many people don't see or realize the hidden truth. It is time to stop fooling ourselves into believing we have it all together. We lie to ourselves by saying that there is no need for deliverance here. Check with someone else who has the appearance of being broken-down. It is time for a real wake-up call. A call invites us to freely open our hearts without fear.

The author takes us on a journey to unlock the spirit of truth by moving beyond the stone, a place where no man dares to go, except he is willing to be free. We cry out to God for help. We wonder why we can't get past certain things in life. Most of the time we are the biggest hindrance in our lives.

Therefore, I challenge you to open your heart, cast down fear and go beyond the stone. Jesus is waiting on you. Take the journey, my friend.

E'donna J.

PREFACE

A couple of years ago, I experienced a devastation that changed my life forever. I lost both of my children in one year. This book is a testament of a divine and very personal account of a sovereign God's delivering power. He saved me from my own deception and happened to wrought out a purpose that he would use as a master tool in His hand to bring you whatever you need.

My daughter, Carrington, was two weeks

from her first birthday and my son, Houston, was stillborn. I buried Carrington. Eight months later Houston was born breathless. At the time, I could not see beyond my own hurt and disappointment. I never imagined that I would be writing this book. I had become so professional at covering my pain that I didn't even realize it. No one could tell that grief was weighing heavily on my heart. I couldn't wait to get home so I could take off my strength and my smile, lie on the floor in the nursery and cry myself to sleep. This went on for almost two years. During that time, I began to convince myself that this was the way it was supposed to be for me. I started satisfying myself with work, using "church duties" to keep myself busy. All the while, deep inside I was embarrassed and disappointed because I felt that God had let me down. He did not show up when I thought he should have.

One day, I was sitting down and (as clear as someone in the room speaking to me) I heard the Spirit of God say, "There is no testimony in saying that what happened was meant to be. The testimony is that you are able to believe me again in spite of what was lost."

Then, He began to show me in the Word His plan was for children and how they are a blessing to the family unit, which is in His perfect will. I had been lured by the enemy into deceiving myself. He used me for my own destruction. When God spoke to me, my eyes were opened. I realized that I was still at the gravesite almost two years after I buried my children. I was living in my past, but God had a whole new plan for my life.

Ever since that day, God has been giving me revelation on this particular text; He also gave me a profound message for you. He saw what happened. He heard you cry. It may seem as if there is no use for Him to answer you now. But, you still need Him. His timing is perfect. Your name has been on the list for some time now. I know you may have thought that He has forgotten you. I'm here to tell you that God has not forgotten you. He is here now to regenerate that hope of being totally free from haunting failures, and to give you a whole new lease on life. Yes, even now He is more than able to raise from the dead every dead thing you have buried. Let's roll away the stumbling blocks at the entrance to the gravesite where all your dead things lay; let's go beyond the

stone.

BEYOND THE STONE

CHAPTER ONE

TRAGEDY AT BETHANY

John 11:1

"Now a certain man was sick, Lazarus of Bethany, the town of Mary and her sister Martha"

1

TRAGEDY AT BETHANY

The town of Bethany was about two miles from Jerusalem. Jesus frequently visited there as he was fond of this city. It was a type of resort for Him. He went to Bethany, not only to relax, but also to see his close friends. They took very good care of Him. They treated Him like family.

BEYOND THE STONE

Jesus was popular and well-respected in Bethany. This city was also the site of many events involving Jesus. This was the place where he taught the popular messages, "The Beatitudes," "The Model Prayer" and "The Great Invitation," which is generally known as "The Sermon on the Mount of Olives." This was the place where He saw the fig tree that had leaves, but no fruit. Jesus said that a fig tree is supposed to have fruit when the leaves are present, but this tree is unfruitful. He cursed the tree at the root, and it dried up. Most importantly, this was the residence of

Martha, Mary and their brother Lazarus. This family hosted Jesus when He came to Bethany.

Lazarus' Dilemma

Lazarus is the brother of Martha and Mary and a very dear friend of Jesus. Out of desperation, his sisters sent an urgent message to Jesus advising him that Lazarus was sick.

Therefore, the sisters sent to Him, saying, "Lord, behold, he whom You love is sick.

- John 11:3

But, when they called for Jesus, He did not come. Jesus stayed where he was for two more days. Lazarus, Jesus' beloved friend, died. Three days later, Jesus still had not shown up.

The people in the town thought that Jesus would surely come quickly because of how He felt about his friend Lazarus. I imagine that people were puzzled and disappointed when Jesus didn't show up. They started talking and murmuring. How could Jesus do this to the person He supposedly loved? How could Jesus do this in the town that respected him so much?

TRAGEDY AT BETHANY

Bethany was His "hang out" place. They had believed that if they were in some sort of trouble, they could call on Jesus and He would come to their rescue. Surprise! This time He did not come.

This passage also alludes to the possibility that Martha and Mary knew the whereabouts of Jesus. They sent a messenger to deliver a message to Him. If they didn't know where Jesus was, they could not have sent a messenger to him. The messenger had to be in a location near Jesus because, not only, did he successfully deliver the message, but also, he returned with one. You don't just deliver a message without getting a response. The Bible does not indicate that there was a confirmation, but we assume that there had to be one. What does that have to with anything?

Well, that would mean that: (1) it did not take the messenger three days to deliver the message; (2) it did not take the messenger three days to return with a confirmation; and, (3) Jesus could not have been far away. So, why did it take Jesus so long to get to His friend? Did Jesus deliberately ignore this message? What was His purpose for doing so?

TRAGEDY AT BETHANY

The last account of the whereabouts of Jesus was east of where John the Baptist baptized.

And He went away again beyond the Jordan to the place

where John was baptizing at first,

and there He stayed.

- *John 10:40*

The area was Perea Bethabara (John 1:28). This area was also right behind the Mount of Olives which ran in the back of Jerusalem, two miles from Bethany. When Jesus traveled to the Mount of Olives, he journeyed in the vicinity of Bethany. This would explain why

Jesus visited Martha and Mary so frequently. The route that He took would lead him to Bethany. He did not have to travel that route, but He did. I believe that He intended to visit His friends as often as He could.

This is the route that He traveled to get to Bethany: (1) Samaria- The Samaritan Woman at the Well (John 4); (2) Galilee- Nobleman's son healed in Cana (John 4:46); (3) Jerusalem- Man with infirmity for 38 years at Bethesda is healed (John 5:6-11); (4) Galilee- Jesus feeds the multitude of 5,000 men not including women and children (John 6:10-14); (5)

TRAGEDY AT BETHANY

Capernaum- Jesus walks on water on the Sea of Galilee (John 6:17-21); (6) Jerusalem- Retribution of the adulteress (John 8:3-12); (7) Jerusalem- Man blind from birth is healed at the Pool of Siloam (John 9:2-11); lastly, Pera- Jesus crossed Jordan and remained for approximately three days where He received the message of Lazarus' illness the first day. Martha and Mary had to have known about Jesus' whereabouts because He was on a crusade. Jesus knew that He would soon be betrayed and crucified for the sins of Man. All of this action could have caused a lot of conversation throughout the area.

You might say people die everyday; why is the death of Lazarus such a tragedy? Because Martha, Mary and Lazarus were friends of Jesus, they must have felt they had priority. They were privileged. Not just that, they fed Jesus and opened their home to Him. He was a special guest in their home. Know this; God will perform one miracle for many reasons. God is efficient like that!

TRAGEDY AT BETHANY

NOTES

BEYOND THE STONE

CHAPTER TWO

THROUGH MARTHA'S EYES

John 11:24

"*Martha said to Him, 'I know he will rise again at the resurrection at the last day.'*"

2

THROUGH MARTHA'S EYES

The sound of the message that was sent to Jesus makes me believe it originated from Martha. The message to Jesus was, "Lord, behold he whom thou lovest is sick." You would have to know Martha's personality to understand why I say this. So, allow me to introduce you to Martha.

BEYOND THE STONE

Details, Details, Details

Our friend Martha was very devoted to everything and everyone she was acquainted with or involved in. Her spiritual relationship with Jesus and her faith were constantly growing. She wished to please, to serve and to do everything right. She really wanted to please Jesus. Although, her major character flaw of being a perfectionist often prevented her from seeing the big picture. Martha was the eldest of her siblings. Oldest siblings have common characteristics. Most are used to taking charge of situations and making sure things get done no matter what the cost. There is no mention of the presence of or absence of parents. So, we can only assume that Martha; being the oldest, took care of her brother and sister.

Martha paid special attention to details. Sometimes, this was to her detriment. She was such a perfectionist that it made others feel uncomfortable. She was a servant from her heart. She cooked, cleaned, and was the most wonderful host to her company. This is evident when Jesus came by for one of his excursions and Martha was busy working like a busy little bee, cleaning, cooking and such.

Where was her sister Mary? She was sitting at the feet of Jesus worshiping Him. Martha, on the other hand, was working feverishly making preparations to ensure that Jesus' stay with them would be perfect.

There was so much work to be done. Martha probably thought her sister had some nerve, enjoying herself, but doing nothing to help. Martha was angered and decided to confront Mary about it. So, she asked Jesus to set her sister straight. The answer Jesus gave her was not quite the one she was expecting.

THROUGH MARTHA'S EYES

He gently corrected Martha by telling her that Mary chose the better part.

Now it happened as they went that He entered a certain village, and a certain woman named Martha welcomed Him into her house. And she had a sister called Mary, who also sat at Jesus' feet and heard His word. But Martha was distracted with much serving, and she approached Him and said, "Lord, do you not care that my sister has left me to serve alone? Therefore, tell her to help me." And Jesus answered and said to her, "Martha, Martha, you are worried and troubled about many things. But one thing is needed, and Mary has chosen that good part, which will not be taken away from her."

- Luke 10:38-42

S.O.S. NEWS FLASH! NEWS FLASH! EXTRA! EXTRA! Read all about it !!!

Let's look at Lazarus' death through Martha's eyes. She and Mary sent an urgent plea to Jesus that he should come quickly because Lazarus was sick. Meanwhile, Martha, in a panicked state, paced the floor, trying to comfort Lazarus and Mary, cooking her brother's last meals, changing the linen on his bed, preparing his grave clothes, helping the physician with his final diagnosis. In frenzy she told the messenger to go find Jesus! Tell him that Lazarus is sick and things don't look well. She said, no, wait! Tell Jesus that Lazarus is coughing uncontrollably, and the physician doesn't know what to do.

The messenger attempted to leave again, but she stopped him. Wait! Scratch that! Tell Jesus that Martha and Mary said that Lazarus is so ill that he is shaking like a leaf, and it doesn't look like he is going to make it through the night. Run! Tell him quickly! Once again the messenger attempted to deliver this ever- so- urgent message. Martha, in all of her turmoil, stopped him again. W-A-I-T !!!!! This is the message I want to send.

BEYOND THE STONE

Tell Jesus, it is "he whom you love is sick." Okay, do you have that? The messenger nodded in amazement while waiting for her to change her mind ... again. She walked away from the messenger and frantically continued pacing. She paused to look back, only to see that the messenger still stood there. She anxiously exclaimed what you are waiting for? Don't you see a man is dying here! The messenger delivered the message to Jesus and returned to Martha to confirm delivery of the message. Well, what did He say? She asked. He hesitantly replied, nothing. By this time

THROUGH MARTHA'S EYES

Martha was beyond belief.

What do you mean, nothing? Are you sure that you talked to Jesus, you know the CHRIST, Son of the living God? I bet you talked to that loud mouth, obnoxious Peter. What did the one you talked to look like? Describe him to me! His feet look like polished brass. His eyes are like fire, his hair like lamb's wool. Did the person you talked to look anything like that? Did you say, Martha and Mary of BETHANY, you know, sisters of HIS friend Lazarus? The frightened look in his eyes, made her realize that maybe the messenger did talk to Jesus. I imagine that Martha sat by the door waiting and waiting for Jesus. Every knock on the door heightened her expectation.

Disappointment gripped her heart every time she answered the door. Finally, what seemed to be the unmentionable became the bitter present reality. Lazarus died. Still, no Jesus.

What she didn't know was that God had a plan for her. He had waited all that time just to unveil what He had created her to become. Martha was going to graduate from servant, to vessel.

From Servant to Vessel

Martha knew what she was good at. She knew how to serve. She was born to serve, so she thought. However, God had another plan. You see, a servant has a will. A servant can choose whether or not they want to be utilized and to what degree they are willing to be used. A servant can say yes or no, but a vessel…that's a totally different story. Martha had been a servant too long. It was time to go to the next level, being a vessel.

Many times, we tell God, "Use me as you

please." But, the moment it becomes uncomfortable we flash the "Off Duty" or "Be Back after This Trial" sign. A vessel is designed to be used, period. You cannot flash either of these signs on. You can't say "No not today, I'm busy." The usage is up to the master or owner of the vessel, not the vessel. This is the lesson she was about to experience. God is about to use her real- life experience to impact a town, the disciples and even their very surroundings. Why, you ask? She had observed Jesus' walk as intimately as the disciples. Now, it was her time to go to the next level of servitude. As far as Martha's eyes could see, her trust in Jesus was limited by what she could see because he had been there for every other crisis that occurred in their lives. He was a frequent guest in their home. She thought she knew Him. She thought she understood Him. All she could see was her brother suffering and his ultimate demise. Facts told her that Lazarus was dead. But the truth of the matter is that it's not over until God said it's over.

Jesus finally arrived four days later, an eternity to Martha.

BEYOND THE STONE

Martha's heart was so wounded that you could almost hear it breaking. He tried to make her see that this was only temporary. Her vision was so impaired that now He looked like an ordinary man. Jesus asked Martha, what happened to you? Haven't you been in my presence all this time? Don't you know when it's too hard for you; it's just right for me? Jesus is not only talking to Martha, but also to you... You walked away from that relationship like there was no hope. You walked away from that bank like their word was final. You walked away from your family like there was nothing else.

Jesus is asking, what happened to you? LOOK IT'S ME! I am not like a normal man that I would lie to you. I won't come back and apologize for anything I promised you. Just because it didn't happen in your timing, doesn't mean that I am through. Lazarus looks dead. I look like an ordinary man. If you look again, you won't see a dead man, you'll see a miracle. Instead of just an ordinary man; you'll see the Resurrection and Life right in front of your very eyes.

BEYOND THE STONE

NOTES

BEYOND THE STONE

CHAPTER THREE

LAZARUS IS DEAD

John 11:14

"Then Jesus said to them plainly, Lazarus is dead."

3

LAZARUS IS DEAD

Lazarus took his last breath; he died. Through the ever-piercing silence, you can hear the heart-wrenching agony Mary and Martha's hearts were experiencing. Grief twisted their faces as they watched the very thing they had believed Jesus for slip from their grasp. Nothing more could be done.

BEYOND THE STONE

Nothing. Lazarus died, their friend, Jesus, didn't show up, didn't call, didn't send a Word.

The spirit of heaviness accompanied by its subtle companion doubt permeated the atmosphere. The spectators said within themselves, I told you they were fools to believe him. What else could Martha and Mary do but bury Lazarus? The crisis was over. Their brother was dead. Now, it seemed as if Jesus didn't care enough to make the graveside service. What would be the use of Jesus showing up now? Lazarus was dead and buried.

Let's take a closer look at some dead things in our lives. Your divorce is final, the money is gone, friends have forsaken you, and have officially declared you worthless. The doctor has given her diagnosis, and the report is bad. Just when you needed them, your so-called friends walked out on you. The job you worked so hard to get and keep is gone. Three years after the disaster, you still haven't put your life back together, and you think you'll never regain all the things you lost. Your children are headed for destruction; you wonder when the nightmare will end. You have asked yourself, how did things get so bad? When did our love lose its sweetness? You have lost someone dear to you, and you don't know how you can go on living.

Many of us have buried dead things in our lives. Those dead things once lived and thrived. We cherished them, and when we were in jeopardy of losing them, we believed that God would come to our rescue.

Now, the thing is dead. You had no choice but to bury it. You were completely embarrassed because you said that God was going to do it for you… and you believed it. But, the thing died anyway. He didn't come through, you think.

The logical thing to do is go into spiritual shock and ignore what has happened to you. You are becoming so "professional" at covering the pain that you are starting to feel numb. You are burying the dead thing in a deep dark place where no one can get to it – not even you. You are putting up a mental block and making yourself forget about it. If anyone asks you about it; you lie and say that you are fine. All the while, you're compacting it deeper and deeper into that cold secluded grave. You are taking your time, wrapping it nicely and neatly in grave clothes so that it won't come back to haunt you. You are putting every memory, and everyone associated with the crisis in a sarcophagus inside the tomb. It isn't working!

Now that you have decided that it is over and done, here comes Jesus. He says; take me to the spot where you have laid that promise down. Jesus is here now. He is calling you to the gravesite, so you can go beyond the stone.

The Spirit of Heaviness

As we walk through this life and experience its changes, disappointments and losses, we sometimes get on ride called an "emotional roller coaster." It always lasts longer than we want it to. The main driving force is depression. People tend to deal with Depression; a symptom, instead of dealing with the root of the problem, the spirit of heaviness. We wonder why after we have prayed about being delivered from this particular spirit, we end up at the doctor's office seeking medical attention. Some ultimately become dependent on various medications for balance to make them feel normal emotionally. This is one of the most common tactics of the enemy.

You see, he doesn't mind you dealing with the manifestations of what is really going on. He enjoys seeing you run after them like a dog chasing his tail. But this day I have come through the power of the Holy Spirit to expose his plan. It's just like a tree that bears fruit.

If you want to destroy the tree, you don't cut off the leaves or the fruit. If you want the tree to die you have to kill the root of the tree. The same principle applies to dealing with any problem or spirit. If you deal with the root of the problem; you can kill the fruit of the problem.

Now in the morning, as they passed by, they saw the fig tree dried up from the roots.

- Mark 11:20

Now in the morning, as He returned to the city, He was hungry. And seeing a fig tree by the road, He came to it and found nothing on it but leaves, and said to it, "Let no fruit grow on you ever again." Immediately the fig tree withered away. And when the disciples saw it, they marveled, saying, "How did the fig tree wither away so soon?" So, Jesus answered and said to them, "Assuredly, I say to you, if you have faith and do not doubt, you will not only do what was done to the fig tree, but also, if you say to this mountain, 'Be removed and be cast into the sea,' it will be done. And whatever things you ask in prayer, believing, you will receive.

- Matthew 21:18-22

The spirit of heaviness is a "kingpin" of its grouping. There are several "manifestations" or spirits that go along with the "kingpin".

Depression is one of the most commonly recognized manifestations. So many people try to alleviate the effects of depression by taking prescription medications. They try to withdraw or isolate themselves from the rest of the world. However, they are merely treating the symptoms of the problem. The root of the problem is the spirit of heaviness. Zoloft, Prozac, sleeping pills of all sorts and other prescription drugs don't resolve the problem. This can lead to chemical dependency, which is yet another problem that compacts the one that presently exists.

Meet the spirit of bondage (another "kingpin") and his cohorts! The spirit of bondage is accompanied by "addiction" and "compulsive drug and alcohol use." The list can go on and on. If you're not careful, pretty soon, you could be the next contestant on "Demon's Gone Wild." You think you are avoiding everyone now, just watch how quickly the tables can turn, and they will start avoiding you. No one wants to be around a constant "pity party."

Get a grip on life! The world is not fair! Things die. Get over it and move on. You have cried long enough. They left ten years ago. The job is gone. The house is gone.

Your children won't listen to your advice. Ten more disasters have devastated the country. Your social-status friends have moved on. The divorce is final. You have played the "blame game" long enough. It has been so long ago, that it doesn't even matter anymore. I have one question for you. "How badly do you want to be free?" Let the Holy Spirit minister to your heart today. Take him to that place where you felt you had no other choice, but to give it up. He is not afraid to go there … are you?

BEYOND THE STONE

NOTES

BEYOND THE STONE

CHAPTER FOUR

STONES

John 11:38

"Then Jesus, again groaning in Himself, came to the tomb.

It was a cave, and a stone lay against it."

4

STONES

Excessive mourning is a doorway that will allow the spirit of heaviness to enter. It is normal to experience a period of mourning after a loss of something or someone dear to you. This is an emotion installed in all of us designed to be a "release valve" for our losses. If the grieving process is not done properly, it can cause psychological dysfunctions.

Here are some examples of the stones, just in case you are wondering if you are harboring one or not: a calloused heart, grief, bitterness, disappointment, hurt, anguish, discouragement, doubt, anger, depression, jealousy, pride and defensive attitude.

Grief

Bitterness, Hurt, Disappointment, Anguish

I'm talking to those of you who are looking for things and people to fill that void in your

STONES

life. People in your life may have died, left you, or just decided that you didn't need them anymore. Now, you are trying to substitute for your loss, and it really is not helping you. It has been going on for such a long time that you've adapted it as a way of life. You've been through a wealth of friendships, relationships, possessions, and ideas trying to fix this, but it is not working. Instead, you are inflicting more pain on yourself and the people around you.

What you don't realize is that you are looking for love in all the wrong places. You are looking for security in things and people when it can only come from God. Jesus is standing there with out stretched arms saying, "I am here. Come to me. Let me make it better." He is a gentleman. He will not impose on you. You have to ask Him to help you.

Take Him to that place where you laid your hopes of healing down. Let him deal with it. Until you let Jesus deal with that hurt, every one of those relationships will fail. You will never be satisfied, and you will die miserable, empty, hurting and still searching.

STONES

Heaven and earth shall pass away, but my word will stand forever.

- *Matthew 24: 35*

They shall perish, but thou shalt endure: yea, all of them shall wax old like a garment, as vesture shalt thou change them, they shall be changed: but thou art the same...

- *Psalms 102: 26, 27*

Hurt

Bitterness, Disappointment

Maybe your spouse or companion has decided that they are simply tired of being with you. Maybe they have decided that they want to *"explore their options"*. Right when you thought you were past the obstacles of separation. All of a sudden, one day they say, I don't want to be with you anymore or I have found someone else.

What then? You thought everything was fine, but evidently it wasn't. You have a choice to make now. You can sit here and cry or you can believe the report of the Lord (Isaiah 53:1). So, what if they are packing or if they have left? Jesus specializes in impossible situations. They may not want to hear you, but they will hear God. It's not over until God says it's over. I don't care if there is no pulse left in the situation, God's Word is final. The Word declares the king's heart is in God's hand and He turns it any way He pleases. What does this mean? It means God is in control. And, if He is in control, everything else is under control.

The king's heart is in the hand of the Lord, as the rivers of the water he turneth it whithersoever he will.

- *Proverbs 21:1*

Discouragement

Pride, Depression, Doubt, Disappointment

You may be out in the deep waters because you stepped out on faith and started that business. You didn't have all the resources you needed but you stepped out in faith. You heard the voice of God and you moved out. Everything was going fine. The clients were coming in left and right. The money was flowing, and you had a full staff. You were able to pay your bills on time and before time. All of a sudden, the clients were at a stand still. The calls stopped coming and the money stopped flowing like it used to. What do you do then?

Is this the same business that the glory was on in the beginning? Are you still as anointed as you were then? You are trying to figure out if you're going to shut it down. You've had to let your staff go because you couldn't afford to pay them anymore. The bill collectors are constantly calling, and the creditors are threatening.

Your friends are saying you're crazy, but God is saying if you hold on to it there is no telling what will come out of it. You're trying to understand how you can hold on to this promise. The devil has been playing with your mind and whispering lies to you saying that God never told you to do this. You're confused in your mind. Depression is making his subtle arrival and you are at your wits end.

You're on the verge of walking away from the business. God has sent me to tell you "don't walk away." It looks dead, but it lives. Its vitality may be undetected, yet it lives. If you walk away, you will have to live the rest of your life in guilt and regret. You may not be able to see your way, still don't let go. You are on the verge of a breakthrough. This trial is not unto death or destruction. It's going to take this experience to make you strong enough to withstand and hold on to the blessings that have been assigned to you. You shall see God's glory! Don't be moved by situations or circumstances when you know what you know He declared from your beginning.

Anger

Defensive Attitude, Disappointment, Grief

BEYOND THE STONE

You may have watched your parents tolerate each other in a loveless marriage up until the time they thought that it wouldn't matter to you anymore. By the time you attained a certain age or reached adulthood or even went away to college, they divorced and crushed everything that would present itself as a loving and meaningful relationship. Now, you're struggling with trust and not resting in the assurance that someone is there for you.

So, you badger them, and you are constantly in a frenzy thinking they are waiting for the opportune time to leave you.

You need to bring that trust issue to God. Take it to that place and lay it bare before Him. Let Him resurrect that trust so you can appreciate the gifts of love that He is placing in your life.

Anguish

Hurt, Pride, Anger

Have you been violated by someone you trusted? Are you uncertain of your sexuality or your self-worth? You are so confused in your mind that you don't know if your identity is male or female. You're making excuses such as, you were born this way. This is a device that the enemy uses to camouflage uncertainty, mental wounds, improperly healed bitterness, anger and rage.

This facade has become a security blanket that shelters you from any further damage to your mind. It gives you a false sense of self-worth as you give a counterfeit account of value in this rigid society. The more the issue is addressed, you allow the real you to be forced further and further in a coma until you are no longer sure which is which.

STONES

If you allow Jesus, He will deliver you. It doesn't matter how long you have been this way. You are not a lost cause as long as there is evidence that you want to be free. There is hope. Let Him set you free to be the person He designed you to be. You may not talk about it openly, but I know that somewhere deep down in your heart of hearts there is a small voice that is crying for help and God has heard it. He has sent this word to deliver you. Be encouraged and allow him to raise your true identity up from the dead.

BEYOND THE STONE

He sent His word and healed them, and delivered them from their destructions.

- Psalm 107:20

Rejection

Calloused Heart, Defensive Attitude

The enemy has deceived you long enough. You have been in and out of meaningless relationships the majority of your life. You thought you had closed this revolving door. You got involved with someone who promised you everything you were searching for, and you bought the lie – hook, line and sinker. Never mind that he or she belonged to someone else. This was your guarantee that you wouldn't have to deal with the surprise of them having other interests. You've lowered your standards and allowed yourself to be satisfied with five hours out of 24 or a visit in the secret of the night while in route to their actual destination. You've settled for the age-old illusion of hope - one day you'll be the only one - but really, it's a mirage. You've accepted a lie the enemy has told you.

He whispers to you that this is all you can

have, or this is all you deserve. You have settled for being a side dish instead of the main course. You've become so comfortable that it's become alright with you, but the devil is a liar! You have been deceived. There is no truth in his words. God says that you are a priority to Him. You are wonderfully made in his image and all He has in mind for you is first class and the best. So, you can tell the devil and his second best offers of affection to forget it! You are the apple of God's eye (Psalm 17:8).

STONES

All of us will face many things in this life, some good and some bad, but all profitable whether we see it or not. Okay, it happened. You tried to forget, but it has come up again. What are you going to do about it? You can't just assume that God will do something about it, but you won't ask Him. Whatever He allows is always for purpose and it is always to help others (Romans 8:28).

Not everything that I have experienced in the past felt good. Sometimes I felt like giving up, but God had all of you in mind. He knew that I needed healing and deliverance. He is using me to write this book for you so that His purpose will be fulfilled. However, He couldn't have done it if I stayed in denial, or tried to go on without allowing Him to deal with my pain and resurrect hope to believe again.

I say to you, take Him to that place where you just couldn't go any further. Allow Him to deal with that dead thing you have forgotten and dare to believe that even now He is able to raise it up again.

STONES

NOTES

BEYOND THE STONE

CHAPTER FIVE

WHERE IS JESUS?

John 10:40

"And He went away beyond the Jordan ... and abode there."

5

WHERE IS JESUS?

Jesus functioned in many gifts, including prophecy. He was the true prophet. He could not only speak things into existence, but he knew what was to come. He knew why He would die. He knew how He would die and when He would die. Lazarus' death and resurrection could have been out of the sequence of events leading up to His purpose had Jesus gone to Judea (Bethany) right away. Jesus had just escaped Jerusalem after preaching a message in the temple that caused a mass bounty on his life. He was right across the Jordan. He was not far, and it appears that He had planned to visit Martha and her family anyway. The route to Jerusalem that Jesus ordinarily took would have allowed Him to visit His beloved friend. In His frequent visits it was on His time. The Jews were waiting to kill Him, but He knew that it was not yet time for Him to go to the cross.

God is not a respecter of persons. Jesus loved Lazarus and his sisters true enough, but he also loved the world and He had a greater task at hand. Jesus understood the significance of time and of His purpose. He knew the value of being at the right place at the right time. Timing is everything! If you step out at the wrong time, things that were meant to be a blessing can become a curse. We will discuss this topic in more detail in the following book, *Crossing Jordan*. No man could take Jesus' life; He said that He would lay it down (John 19:18). This is proof that He was in control of the time and the situation.

We must understand that God is not bound by time. He is eternal. He exists outside of time. The results of our actions and attitudes are reflected in the time spent in our wilderness experience. Once in the wilderness, our journey looks longer and can seem impossible when all hope is lost. However, light can radiate from that same situation if viewed through the eyes of faith. Let's compare Mary and Martha's attitudes and reactions.

WHERE IS JESUS?

It seemed like an eternity to Martha when Jesus finally did arrive. Her reaction to His presence makes that apparent. When she heard that Jesus was on the way, she ran to meet Him where he was. Martha was anxious and merely acting in character.

Now Martha, as soon as she heard that Jesus was coming, went and met Him, but Mary was sitting in the house. Now Martha said to Jesus, "Lord, if you had been here, my brother would not have died."

- John 11:20, 21

Although Martha believed that if Jesus

asked anything of His Father, He would do it for Him; she put limitations on Jesus' deity. Since Lazarus was already dead, she thought the best Jesus could do was to raise him from the dead "in the resurrection at the last day" (John 11:24). She was thinking of the Second Coming of Jesus, but Jesus was talking about the present. Perhaps she did not see the flashing neon "Resurrection" sign on Jesus' chest.

He responded to her:

"I am the resurrection and the life. He who believes in Me, though he may die, he shall live. And whoever lives and

WHERE IS JESUS?

believes in Me shall never die..."

- John 11:25, 26

Let's see how Mary, the worshipper, reacted to Jesus. Upon hearing the news that Jesus was near, Mary sat still (John 11:20). Mary waited on Jesus to arrive and call for her to come to Him.

The word of God says:

"Be anxious for nothing, but in everything by prayer and supplication, with thanksgiving, let your requests be made known to God. and the peace of God, which surpasses all understanding, will guard your hearts and minds through

BEYOND THE STONE

Christ Jesus.

- *Philippians 4:6,7*

Mary had peace. She sat still. She had done all that she knew to do. In her heart, she knew that she would see God's glory whenever Jesus arrived. It didn't matter if it were six seconds, a week, a month, or an eternity. She had seen enough of God's power to know that He was the proven Resurrection. God has done enough for you that He has earned your trust. You have witnessed Him bringing you out of hell. This is a light thing, a simple thing, an easy thing. If you can believe, you will see God's glory.

Martha's attitude lacked worship. Worship was Mary's assurance that Jesus was going to do just what He said. So, stop crying and start worshipping. She believed that even then, Jesus was able to raise Lazarus from the dead. She KNEW that He was the Resurrection and was able to bring life back to their brother, Lazarus.

As morbid as it seems, Jesus was waiting for Lazarus to die. That was the next piece to the divinely orchestrated puzzle so carefully placed together by His Father. It wasn't that

BEYOND THE STONE

Jesus didn't care about His beloved friend. He was waiting for the perfect opportunity to raise an otherwise dead situation. By this time, the disciples were totally confused? They had verified the message delivered by the messenger. The message was that Lazarus, the one Jesus loved was sick; come see about him. The disciples were thinking that Jesus needed to pack His bags and get to Bethany. They were probably ready to pack up and go while the message was being delivered. They thought for sure that Jesus would drop what He was doing to attend to the needs of His "beloved" friend. Much to their surprise, Jesus neither flinched, nor budged. They thought they should help Him comprehend what the messenger said and who it concerned. When Jesus wasn't moved by the message, I'm sure the disciples were baffled. Can you hear them pondering these questions in their hearts: Is Jesus in shock? Has he lost His mind? Hello, didn't you hear that a man is dying? For all they knew, Lazarus could have been taking his LAST breath, gasping for air!

In spite of the urgency of the matter, Jesus simply was not ready. It was not time, yet. He was considerate of the work of His Father and the preparation it took for Him to devise this plan. Timing was everything and everything was dependent upon something else. It's like a domino effect. When one domino falls, the rest fall in sequence.

God knows just when and how to make everything perfect. He is perfect! We, unlike God, have to judge the timing in order to reach a close proximity of perfection; even then, we are no where near perfect.

Jesus also used this opportunity to teach Martha that even though she thought she had exhausted all of her resources, he was still her greatest source. In her mind, she had pulled out her trump card. She had played her best, given her all, pulled all strings. She played what she thought would beat all ... she had sent an urgent plea to Jesus, the Son of God, the Christ, the Resurrection. In spite of her best effort, she walked up on the high joker, the TRUMP OF ALL TRUMPS. Death took Lazarus.

Jesus was not taunting Martha, nor was He trying to discourage her in any way. He wanted her to realize that just because the situation appeared to be over, there was still hope.

> *"... while we do not look at the things which are seen, but at the things which are not seen, for the things which are seen are temporal, but the things which are not seen are eternal*
>
> *-   II Corinthians 4:18*

Everything Is Subject To Change, Even Helpless Situations!

Realize that God has a plan, a surefire strategy that will deliver you out of a dead situation. If Martha had only stuck with her confession, Lazarus would have died, but she would have been at peace, knowing that Jesus was the resurrection. Jesus did not ignore them. He heard them perfectly well. So, why didn't He at least have the common courtesy to send a reply? He had already prophesied that He was the Resurrection. The disciples saw all of the miracles that He had performed. They saw him heal the sick. They saw him **RAISE THE DEAD**. They should have known by His track record that He was equipped to address any situation, in whatever state it was in. They should have told themselves, "Okay, Lazarus died. Wait till Jesus gets here; You WILL live again. Oh yeah! When He gets here, you will live again. You might die, but when He gets here, YOU WILL LIVE!" Everything MUST obey God. Every situation has got to obey His Word when it is spoken in faith. There are no exceptions! It doesn't matter anymore, at that point. If He says that you will not die but live, then you might as well unpack those bags because you're not going anywhere. Fight the good fight of faith! Don't give up! He is coming to attend to your

WHERE IS JESUS?

situation.

BEYOND THE STONE

NOTES

BEYOND THE STONE

CHAPTER SIX

WHAT IS REALLY GOING ON?

John 10:39

"Therefore, they sought again to seize Him, but He escaped out of their hand"

6

WHAT IS REALLY GOING ON?

The Father was establishing Jesus' authenticity as the Son of God. Jesus spoke in a parable that they should eat of His flesh and drink of His blood. That made them think He was a cannibal (John 6: 53-58). He was letting them know that the only way to have eternal life and be with the Father was to partake of Him.

Jesus said to him, "I am the way, the truth, and the life. No one comes to the Father except through Me.

- John 14:6

He taught this in their synagogues. Jesus proclaims that He was the Messiah. That teaching weakened the authority of the Jewish religious leaders. Thus, the Jews plotted to interrupt His crusades, whatever the cost. Everything the people were taught in the Mosaic Law was challenged because Jesus had come to fulfill the law.

In order to fulfill the law, Jesus had to

become the object of the peoples' faith. No longer would they need the High Priest to carry their sins once a year, go through the Holy of Holies advent, nor make another animal sacrifice. Jesus became the High Priest that gave all access to the Father through Himself. What does this all mean? There was no need for the corrupted religious sects. Because of this, the Pharisees, determined to kill him, hunted Jesus and tried to disrupt His ministry (John 7:1).

Mary and Martha knew that Jesus' life was in danger. That's why there was such desperation in their message to Jesus. If Lazarus was sick with a cold, or something minor, they probably would not have sent for Jesus. They would have asked Jesus to just speak the word. They believed and trusted Him. But, this was a crisis, the situation was dire. Lazarus was on his death bed. This was a job for JESUS! Angels, heavenly hosts, were insufficient. They needed JESUS! Jesus knew they were desperate.

He also being a prophet knew that "...this sickness was not unto death". He knew that Lazarus would live again and again. He

WHAT IS REALLY GOING ON?

needed the disciples to understand that even though the Jews were trying to kill Him, that He was exactly who He said He was. They were going to need that very faith that He was instilling in them to carry them through the next series of events. Ultimately, the disciples turned the world upside down because of their faith in Jesus Christ.

They could not do that if they were not fully persuaded. Every person in this passage exhausted his abilities, except Jesus.

After you have kicked and screamed, spent every dime, exhausted all of your resources, seen every psychiatrist, taken all the drugs and drank all of the alcohol you can, Jesus is right there to pick up where you left off. The Father was authenticating Jesus Christ as the Messiah. What Jesus was about to do would establish His deity as being omniscient among other things. He knew the outcome of this crisis.

NOTES

BEYOND THE STONE

CHAPTER SEVEN

THE SHATTERED HEART OF A WORSHIPPER

John 11:32

"Then, when Mary came where Jesus was and saw Him, she fell down at his feet, saying to Him, 'Lord, if You had been here, my brother would not have died."

7

THE SHATTERED HEART OF A WORSHIPPER

If Only You Were Here

Everything was over. Martha was tensed with grief and she told Jesus if He had been here her brother would not have died. Jesus tried to explain that He was there, and He was the resurrection. Martha could not see past what had happened to them and the fact that Jesus had just shown up.

Mary, the true worshipper got it. She had a knack for catching the revelation when no one else did. Remember when Jesus told the disciples that He was going to die. They didn't get it. They were focusing on the things of the natural. Mary caught the revelation and began to anoint Jesus for burial (John 12:1-8). Her perception kicked in again and she believed that even after Lazarus' death that Jesus was able to raise him up from the dead. Jesus' heart was touched by Mary's willingness to give up being in the company of her brother for Him. She bowed down and worshipped Him in the midst of all that was going on. And the Bible says, He wept. Jesus saw her faith and told them to take Him to the place they laid him. Martha replied that they would take Him, but she warned Him that by then Lazarus stinketh. Jesus kept following them and said, "If you can believe, you will see my glory" (John 11:40). He knew He was Lord over the stink.

Take Me to That Spot

Jesus rarely shows up when you want Him. It seems that He is always on time for everything. Isn't that amazing? Some of you are like Martha, looking at your natural situation. You think that it is too late for your marriage to live, it's too late to hope to have children, or it's too late for restoration for your finances or your business. God wants you to take Him to that spot. He says, I am restoration. I am unity. I am the seed and the womb for that child. I am the resurrection. I am waiting to hear you say from your heart, that you know even now I am able to raise this thing up. You may be saying, "Lord, I'm a mess." It has been five, ten or maybe twenty years, but Jesus keeps on coming because He knows that He is Lord over hurt, embarrassment and pain.

Jesus is saying; take me to the place where it got so bad that you didn't want to take it anymore. Take me to where your limitations reached their capacity. Don't worry, He says, I need you to take away the stone of bitterness, hurt, anguish, disappointment, doubt, unforgiveness and anger. I need you to

BEYOND THE STONE

remove your defenses and allow me to deal with that dead promise, that lifeless dream and that forgotten vision that you buried a long time ago, far beyond the stones.

NOTES

CHAPTER EIGHT

BEYOND THE STONE

John 11:39

"Jesus said, 'Take away the stone.'"

8

BEYOND THE STONE

Fear is the stronghold of the enemy. It's used to keep things in the dark.

Its devices are torment, phobias, nightmares, anxiety, distrust, intimidation, deception and embarrassment. These darts of the enemy will hinder you from flourishing and reaching your life's potential. The enemy will plant lies in your mind to deter you from true deliverance. The enemy knows that once you get the truth on the matter, his reign in your life is over. He use deception as the master manipulator to bring on delusions and illusions.

Delusions deal with what you think, and illusions deal with what you see. My friend, whether you believe it or not, your mind plays an important role in the enemy's strategy to destroy you. Your power to BECOME is your mind. The enemy is well aware of this. You will be whatever you think (Proverbs 23:7).

If the enemy can get you to think wrong, he can get you to believe wrong. Whatever you believe you will say (II Corinthians 4:13). As a result, whatever you say, you will have (Mark 11:23). Overcome fear by simply agreeing with the Word. God did not give you the spirit of fear, but of love, power and a sound mind (II Timothy 1:7). God gave you faith, love and a sound mind. Instead of accepting fear, receive the spirit of faith and walk in victory.

BEYOND THE STONE

Take Away the Stone

Jesus followed the mourning sisters through the midst of the crowd, through the spectators and doubters, straight to the place where they had to bear the shame of burying their brother. Mary and Martha walked to the stone with Jesus, who should have saved them from going through this. On the way to the tomb, Martha said, "By this time there is a stench, for he has been dead four days" (John 11:39).

Jesus reminded her of something that He told her previously: if she could believe, she would see the glory of God (John 11:40). Jesus told her that He was not worried about stink. It was exactly as bad as He wanted this situation to be.

Jesus knew that many of the people did not believe that the spirit of man left the body until the third day. So, this was the perfect opportunity to make those who doubted into believers.

Mary, Martha, Jesus and the others, walked to the tomb. Jesus said, "Take away the stone," (John 11:39). The law (custom) at that time required that a person have permission from the family of the deceased before opening an enclosed tomb. This is very important to know, because no matter how badly Jesus wanted to perform a miracle that day, if Mary and Martha had said, No," He would not have. The Bible says, they took away the stone.

I can almost hear the whispering in the background. Jesus lifted His eyes and began to pray aloud to his Father in heaven. He said, "Father, I thank you that you have heard Me. And I know that You always hear Me, but because of the people who are standing by I said this, that they may believe that You sent Me. ... Lazarus, come forth! ...Loose him, and let him go" (John 11:41-44)

I believe the words He spoke in those few seconds caused hell to shake, death to get back and heaven to open up. Every angel on assignment moved. Every demon that was on guard had to bow, drop his weapons and flee. Satan, himself, had to bow and declare that Jesus was Lord on that day.

So, what about you? The stone has been removed and here lies your promise, wrapped in stink, right where you left it. Will you give

Him permission to deal with what's in your tomb?

If you think God is not concerned about you, that He has not received the report of what you have gone through, you are sadly mistaken. Whatever is a concern to you is a concern to Him. He's not worried about it the way you are. God knows that He has a plan. He just wants you to have enough faith to know that He has your best interest at heart. He knows it's a mess. He knows that you almost lost your mind. He knows that without the Word you would have died right along with the vision. You don't have to try to explain to Him or try to prepare Him for the worst. He has seen it all. All He wants you to do is take Him to the place where you gave up. Leave the "stink" up to Him. He knows how long it has been. It's okay. All you have to do is take away the stone and allow Him to deal with this one. When God gets through with this one, those doubters and so-called friends will become believers.

BEYOND THE STONE

NOTES

BEYOND THE STONE

CHAPTER NINE

COME FORTH!

John 11:43

"Now when He had said these things, He cried with a loud voice, Lazarus come forth!"

9

COME FORTH!

Lazarus Come Forth!

Jesus prayed the prayer of faith in the face of that seemingly impossible situation. Then He spoke to *dead* Lazarus and commanded him to come forth. He spoke with such authority that hell had to bow as Lazarus walked out of that grave. I can see the

Holy Ghost at his post, bringing the words that Jesus spoke into existence. Jesus called his name one time and Lazarus got up. The Bible says that he that was dead came forth still bound in his grave clothes. Then, Jesus spoke to the grave clothes, "Loose him and let him go" (John 11:44). Some may disagree here, but I'm going simply by what my Bible says. Some scholars conclude that Jesus told those around to loose Lazarus. Others say, Jesus told the Jews to loose Lazarus. I believe just what the Word says. He didn't say, "Jews, loose him." He didn't say, "Man or women loose him." The Bible simply says, "Loose him and let him go." It is a blessing to me to know that Jesus can speak to whatever is binding me and command it to let me go. Yes, even the grave clothes had to obey that one command.

Loose Him and Let Him Go!

Nobody doubted that the grave clothes would come off. Man could have taken them off, but no one believed that a man who had been dead four days would be raised that day. It would not have made any sense to take off the grave clothes if he were still dead. After

Lazarus was made alive, Jesus demonstrated that even what was binding him had to obey and let him go.

So, I encourage you. Jesus hears your cry and sees your afflictions. He comes to prophesy to that vision, that promise and that dream and command it by the power of the Father to come forth. "Out!" he says from that old stale grave. Don't worry about the grave clothes of bad memories, bad dreams and of what people say or even how you may look believing it again. God says to all of that, "Loose them and let them go." Yes, even your bad memories have to obey the voice of God. Even your past failures are subject to Him.

You see, no one is concerned about you getting rid of or dealing with your bad dreams or past failures. You can go to a psychiatrist for that. But, no one is expecting your vision that was dead to rise up and live again. They are saying, "That's impossible. It's been too long. It cannot possibly be." You need to tell all of hell and the devil, "You thought it was over, but my God has shown up on the scene and declared that it's not going down like that!" As Jesus says, "Come forth!" You reply,

BEYOND THE STONE

"Here I am. I am back!"

COME FORTH!

NOTES

BEYOND THE STONE

CHAPTER TEN

HE THAT WAS DEAD NOW LIVES!

John 12:1

"...*Jesus came to Bethany, where Lazarus was, who had been dead, whom He had raised from the dead.*"

10

HE THAT WAS DEAD NOW LIVES!

Lazarus came forth in the face of all those who doubted andthose who believed. This was an undeniable miracle right before all their eyes. He that was dead now lives. There was nothing they could do about it. They could only stand in awe of the undisputable Son of God. It was a miracle for Mary, a revelation for Martha, proof for the disciples and a warning to the hypocrites that still did not believe.

God will perform one miracle for many reasons. Lazarus was living evidence that could not be contested. Jesus was sent by the True and Living God.

God is speaking to your Lazarus through His Holy Spirit today, and He has commanded it to live. God wants to bring deliverance to you from your past, and He wants to resurrect the very thing that you have given up on. God says, "it can live if you let it." No matter what has happened, who has gone, who hurt you or what you have lost; roll away that stone of unforgiveness, bitterness, pain, jealousy, a defensive attitude and a calloused heart. Let Him command that promise to come forth and live.

II Kings 7: 3-4 (NIV)

> *"Now there were four men with leprosy at the entrance of the city gate. They said to each other, 'Why stay here until we die? If we say, 'We'll go into the city - the famine is there, and we will die. And if we stay here, we will die. So, let's go over to the camp of the Arameans*

and surrender. If they spare us, we live. if they kill us, then we die'."

In this scripture, the men had a choice of staying where they were or moving on. They evaluated their condition and saw that they had nothing to lose. God set them up so that they had more than enough to gain. The one question they asked themselves was, "Why should we stay here until we die?" My question to you is similar. Why should you remain the way you are? You have nothing to lose. Today, God has set you up so that you can gain what He promised you from the start.

It starts with you moving the stone! You may ask, how can I do that? First, you can start by being honest with yourself and God, by acknowledging that stones exist. Secondly, submit them to God, tell Him how you feel, then, ask Him to deliver you. Last, but not least, tell him to let his perfect will be done. When you come to God like this, you shed light on the situation. The devil has to loose you, and deliverance has to come to you. After you have done this, then and only then, will God deal with your Lazarus and cause it to live.

Submission is the key to it all. God says that you have to be willing and obedient to reap the benefits. Willing implies submission. That comes in with your free will and choice to relinquish your will to His. You have nothing to lose, but everything to gain. God is waiting for you to allow Him to go beyond the stone.

HE THAT WAS DEAD NOW LIVES!

NOTES

BEYOND THE STONE

CHAPTER ELEVEN

CONCLUSION

II Kings 7:3

"... Why stay here until we die?"

CONCLUSION

11

CONCLUSION

In every aspect of this journey that we have taken together, there is one constant fact: no matter whose view we were experiencing or whose side of the story we were hearing, God had a purpose-filled plan that was designed for several different reasons.

BEYOND THE STONE

I am here to encourage you. No matter what you have gone through, how long it's been or how difficult it may look or seem, know that God has a plan filled with His divine purpose for your life. He knew when you would go through the crisis, and when you would come out of it. He knew exactly when He would show up and what would happen when he did. You just don't know. He loves you no matter who you are or where you are. God loves you enough to send this little letter to you, to encourage you not to let go of your dreams. If you hold on to it there is no

CONCLUSION

telling what will come out of it.

While going through the sickness and death of my little girl I found myself having to make decisions that I never imagined I would have to make. Some, I am grateful for, some I regret. As I reevaluate that time in my life, I realize that God gave me a message: to cry like one in the wilderness. This message is: Do not base your decisions on what you see because what you see is always subject to change; don't make decisions based on your emotions because they will change; and, you must use your faith to see beyond what you see and press on. The testimony is not that you are learning to deal with things the way that they have ended up, but that you have the power to believe God for the way they could be.

I pray that this book is a blessing to you, and that whatever has been haunting you, from your past, has been defeated through the truth revealed from scripture. In your pursuit of the promise, I trust that this book will continue to teach you the value of submission to God's perfect will for your life. Prayerfully, this will cause you to avoid useless cycles that will make you forfeit or delay your

CONCLUSION

promise. I believe that the pathway to your destiny has been enlightened; your vision has become clearer and your burdens much lighter through this encounter with God. I hope you know Jesus Christ as your personal savior. The only way to true happiness and peace is through Him. If you just believe, He will be whatever you need.

Father, in the name of Jesus, I have done what you have commanded of me. I agree with the Word and the Holy Spirit and I pray for every one who has or will come in contact with this book, that their lives will never be the same.

I believe you Father, that the tactics of the enemy have been exposed and that your people have been made wiser. I cancel every assignment, plan, plot, purpose and trick of the enemy. I take authority over and bind up the spirits of heaviness, bondage and defeat in the name of Jesus and I loose by the power of the Holy Spirit, the garment of praise, the oil of joy for heaviness (Isaiah 61:3), and the work of the Holy Spirit for bondage. Wherever the Spirit of the Lord is there is liberty (II Corinthians 3:17). I loose the spirits

CONCLUSION

of faith, love, power and a sound mind (II Timothy 1:7).

I lift up those who are lost and do not know you and thank you, Father, for allowing this book to be a vehicle that will make their decision to know you easier. I thank you for laborers crossing their path to minister salvation and deliverance unto them. I command the enemy, by the power of the Holy Spirit, to loose their wills so that they may willingly choose to serve Jesus Christ, the only true and risen Savior. I thank you now that even as I pray you have already heard me. Before I cried out to you, you already answered. I thank you Father for healing every wound, pain, bruise, broken heart and mind. I thank you for letting them know that you are truly the balm (medicine) that is needed to heal properly. I thank you that you gave your son Jesus and He gave His blood for this to be so. I thank you for giving them the strength that is needed for them to believe you even after all this time. I thank you that every word that was spoken and agreed upon is so, in Jesus' name. *Amen.*

BIOGRAPHY

Tammie J. Traylor is an anointed vessel of God called to shake the very foundations of hell through the demonstration of the power of the Holy Spirit. She has witnessed the power of God in her life as she has endeavored to fulfill the call and assignment of the Kingdom.

She is a native and resident of Baton Rouge, Louisiana. She is an ordained minister and elder of the Gospel that has dedicated her life to the work of the Kingdom of God. She has received an Associate Degree of Divinity and has been actively involved in the work of the ministry for almost 30 years.

Tammie is anointed to preach and teach the unadulterated word of God. She is a servant of humanity with various philanthropic efforts to assist in making an impact in her community.

She is the founder of Word of Deliverance Ministries Evangelistic Outreach, The F.I.Y.A Covenant Recovery Effort & Center and the Senior Pastor of Word of Deliverance Ministries of Baton Rouge, Louisiana. The woman of God is also a Conference Host, a renowned speaker and traveling evangelist. Tammie also strives to meet the needs of the lost and forgotten by sharing the love of Jesus by any means necessary.

God has anointed her to share the word of deliverance and to bring liberation to broken vessels through the Word of God!